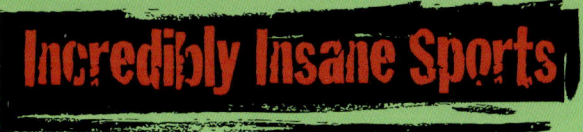

# ROAD CYCLING

By Anne Flounders

Please visit our website, www.garethstevens.com. For a free color catalog of all our high-quality books, call toll free 1-800-542-2595 or fax 1-877-542-2596.

Library of Congress Cataloging-in-Publication Data

Cohn, Jessica.
 Road cycling / Jessica Cohn.
     p. cm. — (Incredibly insane sports)
ISBN 978-1-4339-8835-6 (pbk.)
ISBN 978-1-4339-8836-3
ISBN 978-1-4339-8834-9 (library binding)
1. Cycling—Juvenile literature. I. Title.
GV1043.5.C64 2013
 796.6—dc23
                         2012037750

First Edition
Published in 2013 by
**Gareth Stevens Publishing**
111 East 14th Street, Suite 349
New York, NY 10003

©2013 Gareth Stevens Publishing

**Produced by Netscribes Inc.**
**Art Director** Dibakar Acharjee
**Editorial Content** Anne Flounders
**Copy Editor** Sarah Chassé
**Picture Researcher** Sandeep Kumar G
**Designer** Rishi Raj
**Illustrators** Ashish Tanwar, Indranil Ganguly, Prithwiraj Samat, and Rohit Sharma

**Photo credits:**
Page no. = #, t = top, a = above, b = below, l = left, r = right, c = center
Front Cover: Shutterstock Images LLC  Title Page: Shutterstock Images LLC
Contents Page: Shutterstock Images LLC  Inside: Netscribes Inc.: 10cl, 39b  Shutterstock Images LLC: 4, 5, 6, 7c, 8cl, 8c, 9cr, 10, 11, 12, 13, 14, 15t, 15b, 16, 17, 18, 19, 20, 21, 22, 23t, 23b, 24, 25, 26, 27, 28, 29, 30, 31, 32, 33, 34, 35, 36, 37, 38, 39t, 40, 42.

Printed in the United States of America

CPSIA compliance information: Batch #CW13GS: For further information contact Gareth Stevens, New York, New York at 1-800-542-2595.

# Contents

| | |
|---|---|
| Tough Climbs | 4 |
| The Beginning of Bikes | 10 |
| Built for Speed | 14 |
| All Packed | 18 |
| Building Up | 22 |
| Starting Out | 30 |
| Fast and Famous | 34 |
| Hit the Road | 38 |
| Cycle Speak | 42 |
| Legends of Road Cycling | 44 |
| Glossary | 46 |
| For More Information | 47 |
| Index | 48 |

# TOUGH CLIMBS

One 12,000-foot (3,658 m) climb is a challenge for any cyclist. But there are two such climbs in this part of the USA Pro Cycling Challenge. The course for the day covers 130 miles (209 km). Chilly temperatures, rain, and wind fight against the racers as they push their way up the mountain—twice.

## Flying on the Road

In the USA Pro Cycling Challenge, one cyclist punches down the other side and breaks away from the group. It looks good until another cyclist attacks and **sprints** to the finish. That is just one day of the seven-day race in Colorado's Rocky Mountains, some of the most beautiful and brutal **terrain** for pro cycling.

Colorado's Rocky Mountains provide beautiful but incredibly challenging roads for cyclists.

# Thrill Ride

A slow, steady climb up a hill on a bicycle is rewarded with an electrifying zoom down the other side. It feels almost like flying! That is just part of the thrill of cycling. Millions of people around the world enjoy road cycling. Anyone can take part. Cyclists need only a bike, safety equipment, and an open road.

Cyclists get a feel for how to take curves in the road safely. They are able to do it almost without thinking.

## Why Cycle?

There are 1 billion bicycles on the road throughout the world. People hit the road on bicycles for three main reasons.

**Road cycle racing** is competitive cycling on a road. Roads are often closed off to other traffic for races. People can race in teams or individually. Some races are short and last only a mile or two. Other cycle races are long and take place over several days or weeks. The cyclists do take breaks, though.

**Recreational cycling** is any bike ride done for fun or fitness.

**Utility cycling** is using a bicycle to get from here to there. For example, people ride to work or school on bicycles. It also means cycling for work. In some places, people use bicycles as taxis or for police patrols.

Some people ride bikes for fun. Others use bikes to work. Some police officers patrol on bikes.

These cyclists are taking fun to the next level. They are racing one another. Racing is a chance to show speed and skill on a bike.

## Cycling Across the United States

Cyclists gear up and get racing almost everywhere in the world. The United States is a great place for cycling. Every day, thousands of cyclists push up mountain roads, sail down hills with the wind at their backs, and sprint over the open road. Each year, more and more cities across the United States are making cycling on roads safer for everyone.

Cycling in a group makes cyclists more visible to drivers on the road. But everyone must be aware of dangers such as traffic, animals, and holes in the road.

## Ups and Downs

Different terrain requires different approaches. On flat roads, cyclists shift up into higher **gears**. Then they can pedal fast without losing control of the bike. Going up a hill, **gravity** works against cyclists. Shifting down helps cyclists to push uphill.

# THE BEGINNING OF BIKES

The very first bikes, built in the late 1700s and early 1800s, were not built for speed. They were missing some important parts. No steering and no brakes meant that these bikes were not much fun or much use at all.

Riders sat too high on this "penny farthing" bike for it to be very safe or practical.

This early bicycle, built in 1790, was made of wood. It was not very useful, however. Riders could not steer it. They used their feet to push it along and stop it.

10

## Better Bikes

In 1885, an inventor from England named John Kemp Starley created a bicycle form that is still in use today. His design introduced two wheels of equal size. **Sprockets** and chains at the rear wheel helped move the bike forward. Starley also added inflated tires. They made the ride comfortable and smooth.

The basic design of a bicycle, such as this sprocket-and-chain system, has remained the same since the late 19th century.

## The Test of Time

Cyclists ride bikes very similar to late 19th-century machines. The top cycling athletes in the world still compete in many of the same races as cyclists did 75 to 100 years ago. For example, the Tour de France was first raced in 1903. Cycling has been an event in the Olympic Games since 1896.

In 1894, women began wearing bloomers. Bloomers are underwear that look like pants. Bloomers allowed women in skirts to ride more easily on bikes.

## Cycling Through History

**1868** The first recorded bicycle race took place in Paris, France. An Englishman named James Moore won on his wooden bike. The race was about 0.75 mile (1.2 km) long.

**1885** John Kemp Starley of England built the "safety bicycle." Its basic design is still used today.

**1896** The first modern Olympic Games were held in Athens, Greece. Bicycle racing was one of the events.

**1903** *L'Auto*, a French newspaper, sponsored the first Tour de France.

**1914** Mass production of bicycles began, which meant that many were made at one time. This meant that more people could afford them.

# BUILT FOR SPEED

Road cycles are made for the road. Their basic structure is the same as off-road bikes. But only road bikes have handlebars that curve down. On a road bike, the cyclist leans over to grasp the handlebars. Doing so allows the wind to race over the cyclist's back. Then the cyclist can tear through the course at top speeds.

Hill climbs are tough. Toward the top, cyclists get into a standing position so their body weight helps push down on the pedals.

## Rubber Meets the Road

In a road cycle race, speed is king. When the tire of any bicycle meets the road, the tire flattens slightly. The more tire surface on the road, the slower the bicycle goes. That is why road cycles have narrow tires. Racers also make sure their tires are inflated properly for the road. A tire that does not have enough air can slow a racer down. Too much air in the tire makes for a bumpy ride.

Cyclists can change positions throughout a ride to avoid feeling sore in any area of the body.

## TEST IT!

Racing cyclists depend on **aerodynamics** to help them move fast. Aerodynamics are the way that air moves over a cyclist's body and bike. Leaning forward allows air to move more quickly over a cyclist, so the cyclist zooms faster. Test this with a paper airplane. Throw a paper airplane with its nose pointing forward, so the plane goes straight ahead. Then throw the same paper airplane straight ahead with the same force, but with its nose pointing up in the sky. How do the two flights compare?

15

## Totally Tubular

For nearly a century, most racing bikes were made of steel tubing. Some bikes were also built with aluminum and titanium **alloys**. An alloy is a mixture of metals that together create a stronger metal. Titanium is a very strong but light metal. Hollow tubes made of light metals help a bicycle move nimbly over roads and curves and up hills. Today, most racing bicycles are made of carbon fiber, which is even lighter than metal.

Cycle racing rules are set by an international organization called UCI. Its rules say that racing bikes can be no lighter than 14.99 pounds (6.8 kg). But the new carbon fiber racing bikes are much lighter than the metal cycles that were used when the rule was made. Officials are considering changing the rule.

**Bike Materials: Pros and Cons**

|  | Carbon Fiber | Steel | Aluminum Alloy |
|---|---|---|---|
| Pros | Super lightweight | Strong | Lightweight |
|  | Will not rust | Durable | Good for racing |
|  | Gives a smooth ride | Not too expensive |  |
| Cons | Expensive | Could rust in wet conditions | May rust |
|  | Not easily repaired |  | Not as long-lasting as other materials |

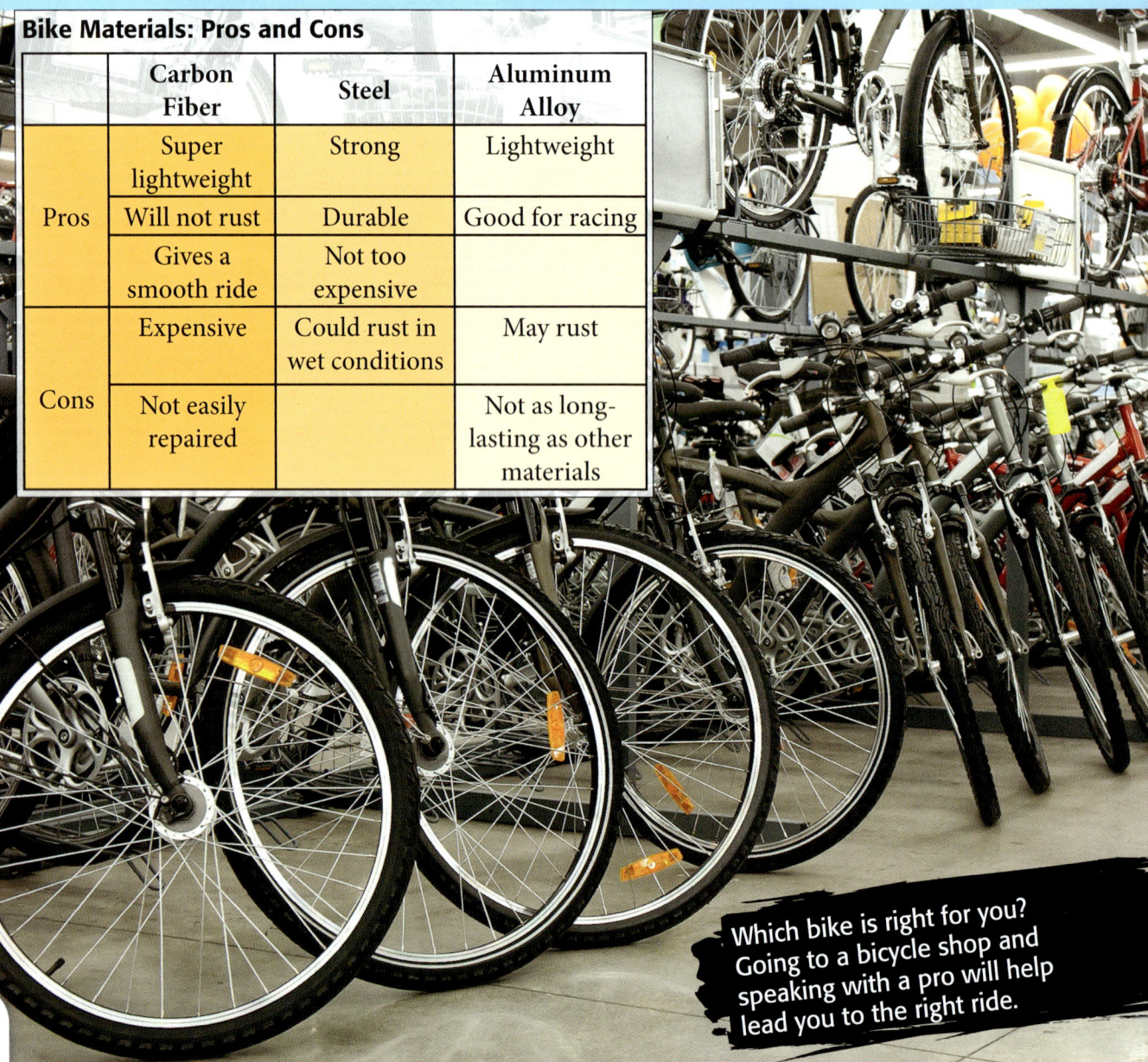

Which bike is right for you? Going to a bicycle shop and speaking with a pro will help lead you to the right ride.

## Shifting Gears

As a cyclist rides, he or she will shift gears depending on whether the bike is going uphill, downhill, straight, or around a corner. Gears help the cyclist keep the speed of pedaling, or the **cadence**, steady throughout the ride. Gearshifts on the handlebars of a bike are connected to gears on the front and back wheels. Some cyclists now use new electronic gear-shifting systems.

Going uphill can be tough. Shifting down to a lower gear can help a cyclist pedal ahead.

# ALL PACKED

When racing, most riders are in a pack called a **peloton**. The cyclists ride very close to one another. They must take care to avoid crashing into each other's bikes. Safe riders avoid sudden, unexpected movements and "hold the line." That means they travel in a straight line and do not drift into anyone else's path. That is a fast way to bring down a pack of cyclists.

The term "peloton" is also a general term referring to any group of pro cyclists.

## Safe Pedaling

The thrill of road cycle racing comes with risks. Every move one cyclist makes will affect the other racers in the group. "On your wheel!" a cyclist might shout if his or her front wheel nears the rear wheel just ahead. But even the most careful riders can meet an unexpected road **hazard**. Quick thinking is just as important as following the rules of the road.

Expert cyclists keep their hands on their handlebars and try to land on their sides when their bikes tip over.

## Gear Up

A racing cyclist wants to concentrate on the ride, not on painful blisters or rashes. Cyclists wear special clothes when they hit the road. Bike shorts and jerseys are made of a tight-fitting material such as Lycra, which allows the air to move freely over the rider. That helps the bike go faster. Bike shorts and jerseys do not have seams, which could rub against the skin. The shorts have padded bottoms for extra comfort.

Cyclists are on the go all year long. In cold weather, cyclists wear layers of special clothing to keep warm and dry. The clothing fits snugly so it doesn't slow them down or get caught in the bike.

## Neat Feet

Cycling shoes are sneakers with stiff bottoms, which help transfer power from the rider's foot to the bike's pedal. Cycling socks keep moisture away from cyclist's feet and prevent blisters.

20

## Head of the Pack

Every cyclist needs a good helmet to protect his or her head from injury. Cycling glasses protect a cyclist's eyes from wind, sun, dirt, gravel, and bugs.

A helmet should fit correctly. It should not be too loose or too tight.

## TEST IT!

Bicycle shoes have stiff soles. Soft soles do not transfer power from a rider's feet to the pedals easily. That is because they absorb, or take in, energy. Hard soles allow energy to go more quickly to the pedal. Test this at home. Sit in a chair on a flat, hard surface, in front of a wall. Use the flat surface of a hardcover book to help push against the wall and move your chair back. Next, try moving the chair by pushing a soft pillow against the wall. Which is easier?

21

# BUILDING UP

A cyclist needs to stay strong. **Aerobic** exercise helps build **stamina** for long rides. Eating nutritious food for energy and getting enough sleep to stay alert help riders jam hard on the road. Drinking enough water helps keep the body healthy and strong, too.

## Core Conditioning

A cyclist takes a tight curve and leans into it. Amazingly, the cyclist does not fall over. That is a cyclist who has great control over his or her bike. Much of that control comes from having a strong core. Those are the muscles in the center of the body, including the abdomen, back, sides, and hips.

Cyclists stay strong and fit by lifting weights, running, and doing other types of exercise.

## TEST IT!

Want to feel your own core get stronger? Try this exercise. Lie with your stomach and knees on the floor. Prop yourself up on your elbows. Lift up your knees so that your feet, forearms, and elbows are the only parts of you touching the floor. Do you feel your muscles working to keep you straight and your body off the floor? That is your core!

## Against the Wind

In the beginning of a race, cyclists keep together in a peloton. They do not do this just for company. It is a smart racing tactic. A cyclist riding alone rides against the wind. That quickly tires a cyclist out. So cyclists take advantage of **drafting**. That is a method of saving energy by riding behind other riders. The rider or riders in front work the hardest. After a while, they switch places with the riders behind them. Everyone takes turns working the hardest so no one gets worn out.

Wind resistance is especially strong on flat surfaces. When a group moves up a hill, everyone is moving more slowly, so the wind resistance is weaker.

## TEST IT!

See for yourself what drafting is like. Place both hands, side by side, in front of a fan. Then move one hand behind the other. If your hands were bikes, the hand in back is the one in the **slipstream** while most of the air hits the hand in front.

Sprinting is a burst of speed at the very end of a race.

## Breaking Away

There are times when a rider wants to break away from the group and get ahead. This might be while the riders are going up a hill. Riders also break away for the final speedy sprint toward the finish line.

# Race to the Finish

Road cycling races can be individual or team races. A criterium is a race on a short, closed road circuit, or loop. Cyclists circle the loop a number of times. In a time trial, cyclists start individually to cover a set distance as fast as possible. A road race is a race from one point to another. All the cyclists begin the race together in a peloton. In a hill climb, the finish line is uphill from the starting point. A multistage race is a collection of individual races that take place over the course of several days or weeks. The winner is the person who has the fastest time after all the races.

A caravan follows the racers. It may carry race officials, coaches, people who help sick or hurt cyclists, and people who can fix the bikes.

# The Cream of the Crop

Imagine getting on a bike and racing some of the best cyclists in the world. Now imagine racing for three weeks over 2,100 miles (3,380 km). Such a race happens every year. The Tour de France is one of the world's greatest sporting events. Millions watch as cyclists push themselves up high mountains and zoom around tight curves in the roads in this multistage race.

Each day, the current leader of the Tour de France wears a special yellow jersey. This makes it easy for the other riders to see the one they need to beat.

## Going for Gold

Cycling has been a part of the Olympic Games since the beginning. The first modern Olympics were held in Athens, Greece, in 1896. Cyclists raced on a 54-mile (87 km) course from Athens to Marathon and back. The gold medal went to Aristidis Konstantinidis of Greece. He won despite the fact that his bike broke down on his ride back to Athens.

### TEST IT!

In the 2012 Olympic Games in London, women rode a course that is about 87 miles (140 km) long. If a cyclist completed the race in exactly three and a half hours, what is the average speed she traveled?

Answer: About 24.9 miles (40 km) per hour

Cycle racing is an event in the Summer Olympics. These games are held every four years in a different country.

28

## Welcome, Women!

Although women are no strangers to competitive cycling, they did not compete in the Olympic Games cycling events until 1984. That year, the gold medal went to Connie Carpenter of the United States.

**Great Riders**
These countries earned medals in road cycle racing in the last six Summer Olympic Games.

| Country | Number of Medals in the Summer Olympics (1992–2012) | Country | Number of Medals in the Summer Olympics (1992–2012) |
|---|---|---|---|
| United States | 8 | Australia | 2 |
| Germany | 7 | Canada | 2 |
| Russia | 7 | Sweden | 2 |
| Great Britain | 7 | Belgium | 1 |
| Netherlands | 6 | Denmark | 1 |
| Switzerland | 5 | Latvia | 1 |
| France | 4 | Lithuania | 1 |
| Italy | 4 | Colombia | 1 |
| Spain | 3 | Portugal | 1 |
| Kazakhstan | 2 | Norway | 1 |

# STARTING OUT

Racing cyclists start out by simply riding—a lot. When a cyclist feels ready to start racing, it is just a matter of signing up for a race. Cycle racing has five categories. Beginning racers start out in Category 5. As they participate in more races, they move up through the categories. The fastest, most experienced racers are Category 1.

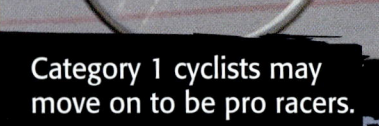

Category 1 cyclists may move on to be pro racers.

# Head of the Class

Racers compete against others in their own class. A class is determined by the age of the racer. This chart shows the ages and classes for cycle racing in the United States.

| Racing Age | Class |
|---|---|
| Under 10 | Youth |
| 10–18 | Junior |
| 19–22 | Under 23 |
| 23–29 | Elite |
| 30 and above | Master |

Some juniors have the chance to take part in international racing trips. They ride in big junior cycling events during the summer.

# The Hub of the Wheel

USA Cycling is the central organization for competitive cycling in the United States. It began in 1920 as the Amateur Bicycle League of America. The group became USA Cycling in 1995. Riders, coaches, **mechanics**, and race officials are all part of this organization. Anyone can join a local USA Cycling club. Once a cyclist joins, he or she can get right into racing.

To participate in a race, a cyclist needs to sign up with USA Cycling.

## Join the Club

Across the nation, USA Cycling runs 2,500 clubs and teams. People join their local cycling clubs. They train and race together. USA Cycling had 70,829 **licensees** in 2011. That is 66 percent more than it had in 2002. The sport is gaining in popularity.

### What Do You Think?

Why do you think cycle racing is so popular across the United States?

Clubs and teams have regular training rides. It's a great way to learn to cycle in a group and to make new friends.

# FAST AND FAMOUS

As long as there have been bicycles, there have been cycling stars. The first was James Moore. He won the very first cycle race, which was held in Paris in 1868. Moore was 19 years old. The course was about 0.75 mile (1.2 km) on a rocky path. Moore went on to win more races, including the first Paris–Rouen race. He covered 81 (130 km) miles in a bit over 10 hours. That is just eight miles per hour. Pro racing cyclists today average speeds of 21 to 28 miles (34 to 45 km) per hour.

## A New Direction

Kristin Armstrong started her athletic career as a **triathlete**. But she began to have bad pain in her hip. The pain was arthritis, a disease of the joints. She could no longer run. From then on, Armstrong threw her energy into cycling, which her doctor said was better for her hips. She went on to win a gold medal in the 2008 Olympics. The medal is just one of many first-place finishes for this champion athlete.

The key to riding well is listening to one's own body. Pro cyclists train hard to ride as fast as they do. Casual or new riders should go at an easier pace.

## Terrific Times

Do not blink or you will miss David Zabriskie. He is one of the speediest time trial cyclists in the world. In 2005, he set a record for riding the fastest time trial at the Tour de France. When Zabriskie's not training or racing, he is often found online. He is a popular blogger and Twitterer.

Riding in a group is a skill. Cyclists learn to go with the flow of the group and to find their best position within the group.

# Yield to Life

David Zabriskie's career was almost ended by an SUV. In 2003, Zabriskie was riding on the road in his hometown of Salt Lake City, Utah, when an SUV made a left turn and hit him. He was in a wheelchair for months. His doctors thought he might not ride again. Hard work and determination put him back on the bike. Zabriskie later started Yield to Life, an organization that teaches motorists and cyclists to share the road safely and respectfully.

Both cyclists and motorists must obey the rules of the road.

# HIT THE ROAD

Ready to ride? First, make sure you have a bicycle that fits you. Bicycles come in different sizes and have adjustable seats. A cycle shop pro can help you get set up properly. Always wear your helmet. It is your most important piece of safety equipment. Review the rules of the road before you go.

## Rules to Go

There are some very basic but important rules of the road to follow when riding a bicycle. Stay on the right side of the road. Stop at red lights and stop signs. Don't weave back and forth. Pedal steadily ahead for a safe ride.

### Give Us a Hand
Hand signals show motorists and other cyclists what you are doing next in your ride. The chart below shows the signals to use.

| Left turn | Right turn | Stop |
|---|---|---|
|  | or |  |

Smart cyclists think ahead. They make good guesses about what drivers, walkers, and other cyclists will do next.

## Get Going

Anyone who is comfortable on a bicycle can learn to race. As with any sport, it takes time to build speed and strength. Strap on your helmet, find a safe course, and practice hill climbs and speedy sprints. Cyclists who want to take it to the next level can join a local cycle club to start racing.

# Ready for a Ride
Once a young cyclist understands road safety, some basic gear is needed.

**a brightly colored shirt**
*Bright colors are easy to see on the road. Reflector tape can also be added to a shirt.*

**bicycle**
*Make sure it fits. A bike shop pro can recommend the right size. The bicycle should have good **reflectors** so that people can see the bicycle easily. Reflectors shimmer when light hits them.*

**helmet**
*A helmet is a must. It needs to be fitted properly, too.*

**gloves**
*Gloves can prevent blisters on hands. They can also protect hands in case of a fall.*

**sturdy shoes**
*Leather sneakers with Velcro instead of laces are a good choice for getting started in cycling.*

**bicycle pump**
*For a safe and smooth ride, tires must be pumped up and solid.*

41

# CYCLE SPEAK

Watch out for Fred and Doris. That is "cycle speak," or cycling lingo, for people who are new to the road. As in other sports, there is a special language that is shared by the people who enjoy road cycling. Not surprisingly, a lot of the language has to do with speeding ahead.

## Words of the Road

Do you want to talk the talk of road cycle racers? To *attack* is to speed up quickly and leave daylight between you and the other riders. A *breakaway* is a successful attack. A *kick* is a quick, hard acceleration.

## Words in Context

**Can you guess the meaning of these road cycling words and phrases?**

1. Do not be a *wheelsucker* or a *leech*. Get to the front of the group and take your turn.

    *wheelsucker or leech: a person who does not take his or her turn riding at the front of the group and doing the hardest work*

2. She was *off the back* as the peloton pulled ahead.

    *off the back: behind the pack*

3. He was cruising along, *pedaling circles* and enjoying the view.

    *pedaling circles: pedaling smoothly*

4. That cyclist must be exhausted. He is *pedaling squares*.

    *pedaling squares: having a tough time pedaling*

5. The *roadie* knew all the best biking routes, and she sailed up hills like they were flat land.

    *roadie: a serious road cyclist*

# LEGENDS OF ROAD CYCLING

The legends of road cycling are men and women whose skills and speed won attention and awards. Some were pioneers of the sport, and many were record breakers.

## Five Famous Racers

In 1995, **Fred Rompelberg** of the Netherlands broke a speed record when he went 167 miles (269 km) per hour on a flat surface.

**Greg Kolodziejzyk** of Canada raced 647 miles (1,041 km) in 24 hours, which broke a distance record in 2006.

French cyclist **Barbara Buatois** raced 75 miles (121 km) per hour on a flat surface in 2010. This broke a speed record for women.

In 2012, **Seana Hogan** rode nearly 446 miles (718 km) in 24 hours. Hogan is a female American cyclist.

## Behind the Legends

The best road cycle racers compete in races that take them to some of the most beautiful places in the world. Here are six of the most famous road races. Some of these races are more than 100 years old.

| Name | Type of Race | Year First Held | Country | Description |
|---|---|---|---|---|
| Giro d'Italia | multistage | 1909 | Italy | This race is often called "The Giro." Each day the cyclist with the fastest overall time wears a pink jersey. |
| Giro di Lombardia | road race | 1905 | Italy | This road race takes place in the fall. Its nicknames are "the race of the falling leaves" and "the climber's classic." |
| Milan–San Remo | road race | 1907 | Italy | Often called "the sprinter's classic," it is the longest professional one-day race at just over 185 miles (298 km). |
| Tour de France | multistage | 1903 | France | In this three-week race, the course changes every year, but it always ends in Paris. |
| Tour of Flanders | road race | 1913 | Belgium | This race takes cyclists up and down many sharp hills and over cobblestone roads. |

## Race to Know

Who are some of the great racers in cycling today? This list names a few of them. Use the library, and the Internet, to find out about each person's accomplishments and home country.

| | | |
|---|---|---|
| Alejandro Valverde | Giorgia Bronzini | Robin Farina |
| Bradley Wiggins | Jens Voigt | Samuel Sánchez |
| Emma Johansson | Marianne Vos | Tatiana Guderzo |
| Emma Pooley | Mark Cavendish | Taylor Phinney |
| Evelyn Stevens | Nicole Cooke | Timothy Duggan |

# Glossary

**aerobic:** relating to oxygen

**aerodynamics:** science of the motion of air and the forces acting on bodies exposed to air

**alloys:** mixtures of metals used to make a bicycle

**cadence:** pedaling rhythm

**drafting:** riding closely behind another rider, so that the rider in front is doing most of the work of riding into the wind

**gears:** parts on a bicycle that determine the speed the cycle will go

**gravity:** attraction between objects that have mass

**hazard:** source of danger

**licensee:** group or person holding a license, which is a paper showing permission to do something

**mechanics:** people who repair vehicles and other machines

**peloton:** a group of cyclists

**reflectors:** surfaces that throw back the light that hits them

**slipstream:** in drafting, the area behind the lead rider where it is easier to ride

**sprints:** pedals fast, especially at the end of a race

**sprockets:** toothed wheels whose teeth fit into the links of a chain

**stamina:** ability to keep making a physical effort

**terrain:** physical features of land

**triathlete:** person who competes in a race that includes cycling, running, and swimming

# For More Information

## Books
Brill, Marlene Targ. *Marshall "Major" Taylor: World Champion Bicyclist, 1899–1901*. Minneapolis, MN: Twenty-First Century Books, 2007.

Graham, Ian. *The Science of a Bicycle.* Pleasantville, NY: Gareth Stevens, 2009.

Kelley, K.C. *Stunt Bicycle Riding.* Milwaukee, WI: Gareth Stevens, 2004.

Pease, Pamela. *Pop-Up Tour de France: The World's Greatest Bike Race.* Chapel Hill, NC: Paintbox Press, 2009.

## Websites

### Bicycling Magazine
*www.bicycling.com*
The site has news, reviews, and more from the word of cycling.

### CYCLE Kids
*www.cyclekids.org*
This site introduces kids to the joys of cycling.

### KidsHealth
*kidshealth.org/kid/watch/out/bike_safety.html*
Don't hit the road without reading this first.

**Publisher's note to educators and parents:** Our editors have carefully reviewed these websites to ensure that they are suitable for students. Many websites change frequently, however, and we cannot guarantee that a site's future contents will continue to meet our high standards of quality and educational value. Be advised that students should be closely supervised whenever they access the Internet.

# Index

aerodynamics 15
Armstrong, Kristin 35
Athens, Greece 13, 28

bicycle 5, 6, 7, 11, 13, 14, 15, 34, 38
brakes 10
Buatois, Barbara 44

Carpenter, Connie 29
chains 11

drafting 24, 25

England 13

gravity 9

helmet 21, 38, 40
hill climb 14, 26, 40
Hogan, Seana 44

Kolodziejyk, Greg 44
Konstantinidis, Aristidis 28

Moore, James 13, 34
multistage race 26, 27, 45

Olympic Games 12, 13, 28, 29, 35

Paris, France 13, 34, 45
Paris–Rouen race 34
peloton 18, 24, 26, 43

recreational cycling 6
road cycle racing 6, 19, 29
road race 26, 45
Rompelberg, Fred 44

safety 5, 8, 10, 13, 18, 19, 37, 38, 39, 40
shift 9, 17
shoes 20, 21
slipstream 24, 25
speed 10, 14, 17, 25, 28, 34, 36, 40, 42, 44
sprint 4, 8, 25, 40, 45
sprockets 11
Starley, John Kemp 11, 13
steering 10

terrain 4, 9
time trial 26, 36
Tour de France 13, 27, 36, 44, 45

United States 8, 29, 32
USA Cycling 32, 33
USA Pro Cycling Challenge 4
utility cycling 6

Yield to Life 37

Zabriskie, David 36, 37